Mastering Generative AI Software

Development

Table of Contents: Generative AI Software Development

Part 1: Introduction to Generative AI

Part 1: Introduction to Generative AI

This section dives into the world of Generative AI, exploring its core concepts and applications. We'll begin by understanding what generative models are and how they differ from traditional machine learning approaches.

Chapter 1: What is Generative AI?

- **1.1 Understanding Generative Models:**
  - In this section, we'll unpack the concept of generative models. We'll delve into how they learn from existing data to create entirely new and original content, be it text, images, code, or even music.

- We'll explore the key distinction between generative and discriminative models, commonly used in machine learning. Discriminative models learn to classify or predict based on existing data, while generative models go a step further by creating entirely new examples that resemble the training data.

- **1.2 Applications of Generative AI:**

  - Here, we'll uncover the exciting potential of generative AI across various domains. We'll explore its applications in creative fields like generating realistic images, composing music, or writing different kinds of creative text formats.

- Beyond creative endeavors, generative AI finds its use in scientific research for tasks like drug discovery and material design. We'll delve into some real-world examples to showcase its versatility.

- **1.3 Benefits and Challenges of Generative AI:**

  - This section will discuss the numerous benefits generative AI brings to the table. We'll explore how it can automate tasks, accelerate creative processes, and even aid in scientific discovery.

○ However, generative AI also comes with its own set of challenges. We'll discuss potential biases that can creep into models, along with issues like copyright and the ethical implications of creating highly realistic content.

Chapter 2: Core Concepts in Generative AI Development

- **2.1 Machine Learning Fundamentals for Generative AI:**

- Before diving into generative models themselves, we'll establish a foundation in core machine learning concepts. This section will cover essential topics like neural networks, loss functions, and optimization algorithms.

- Understanding these fundamentals will be crucial for grasping how generative models work and the training process involved.

- **2.2 Types of Generative Models (Generative Adversarial Networks (GANs), Variational**

Autoencoders (VAEs), Autoregressive Models):

- Now that we have a grasp of machine learning basics, we'll delve into the different types of generative models.

- This section will introduce you to some of the most popular architectures, including Generative Adversarial Networks (GANs), Variational Autoencoders (VAEs), and Autoregressive models.

- We'll explore the working principles of each model, highlighting their strengths and weaknesses, along with the kind of

data they are best suited for.

- **2.3 Evaluation Metrics for Generative Models**

  - Evaluating the effectiveness of a

    generative model is crucial. Here, we'll

    discuss different metrics used to assess

    the quality of generated outputs.

  - We'll explore metrics that measure

    realism, diversity, and adherence to the

    training data.

By the end of Part 1, you'll have a solid

understanding of what generative AI is, its various

applications, and the core concepts that underpin

its development. We'll have established a foundation for exploring how these models are built and implemented in the following chapters.

Part 2: Building Generative AI Systems

Part 2 dives into the practical aspects of building generative AI systems. Here, we'll explore the data preparation process, delve into model design and training, and uncover advanced techniques that can push the boundaries of generative AI development.

Chapter 3: Data Preparation and Preprocessing for Generative AI

- **3.1 Data Requirements for Different Generative Models:**

- Generative models, like all machine learning approaches, are heavily reliant on data. This section explores the specific data requirements for different generative model architectures.

- We'll discuss factors like data size, format, and quality essential for successful model training.

- For instance, generating realistic images might require vast datasets of labeled images, while text generation models might thrive on large amounts of text corpora.

- **3.2 Data Cleaning and Augmentation Techniques:**

  - Real-world data is rarely perfect. This section explores data cleaning and augmentation techniques crucial for preparing high-quality training data for generative models.

  - We'll cover methods for handling missing values, outliers, and noise in the data. Additionally, we'll delve into data augmentation techniques that artificially expand the dataset, improving model robustness and performance.

Chapter 4: Designing and Implementing Generative AI Models

- **4.1 Choosing the Right Generative Model Architecture:**

- With a foundation in data preparation, we'll now explore the design considerations for generative models. This section delves into choosing the right generative model architecture for your specific task.

- We'll revisit the different types of generative models introduced in Part 1 (GANs, VAEs, Autoregressive models) and discuss their strengths and weaknesses in different scenarios.

- We'll explore factors like the nature of your data, desired output format (text, image, etc.), and the trade-offs between

model complexity and performance to

guide your selection.

- **4.2 Training Generative AI Models (Loss**

Functions, Optimizers):

  - Generative models require extensive

    training on prepared datasets. Here, we'll

    delve into the training process, including

    the use of loss functions and optimizers.

  - Loss functions quantify the difference

    between the model's generated outputs

    and the desired outcome. We'll explore

different loss functions used for generative models.

- Optimizers are algorithms that iteratively adjust the model's internal parameters to minimize the loss function. We'll discuss popular optimizers used for training generative models.

- **4.3 Monitoring and Debugging Generative Model Training:**

  - Training generative models can be a complex process. This section explores techniques for monitoring and debugging the training process.

- We'll discuss how to visualize training progress, identify issues like overfitting or underfitting, and implement strategies to fine-tune the training process for optimal results.

Chapter 5: Advanced Techniques in Generative AI Development

- **5.1 Generative Pre-training Models:**
  - Generative pre-training models are a recent advancement that has significantly boosted the capabilities of generative AI.

This section explores the concept of pre-trained models and their role in generative AI development.

- ○ We'll discuss how pre-trained models learn generic representations of data that can be leveraged by downstream generative models, leading to improved performance and efficiency.

- **5.2 Prompt Engineering for Generative AI:**

  - ○ Prompt engineering is a powerful technique for guiding the output of generative models. This section explores how crafting effective prompts can significantly influence the quality and direction of the generated content.

- We'll delve into strategies for formulating clear, concise, and informative prompts that steer the model towards the desired outcome.

- **5.3 Explainable AI (XAI) for Generative Models:**

  - Generative models can be complex "black boxes." This section explores the concept of Explainable AI (XAI) and its application to generative models.

- We'll discuss techniques for understanding how generative models arrive at their outputs, fostering trust and enabling better control over the generated content.

Part 3: Applications of Generative AI Software

Generative AI is no longer confined to research labs. This part explores the exciting and diverse applications of generative AI software across various industries.

Chapter 6: Generative AI for Creative Content Generation

Generative AI is revolutionizing creative fields, empowering artists and content creators. Here, we'll delve into how generative models are transforming creative content generation.

- **6.1 Text Generation (Poetry, Code, Scripts):**

  - Unleash your inner writer! Generative AI can craft poems, scripts, and even code. We'll explore how models can generate different writing styles, helping writers overcome writer's block or brainstorm new ideas.

  - We'll also discuss the potential of AI-generated code for automating repetitive tasks and accelerating software development.

- **6.2 Image and Video Generation (Art, Design, Animation):**

  - Generative AI is pushing the boundaries of visual arts. We'll explore how models can create stunningly realistic images, generate unique design elements, and even produce short animations.

  - This opens doors for artists to explore new creative avenues and for design professionals to streamline their workflows.

- **6.3 Music Generation:**

- Get ready for a symphony composed by AI! Generative models can create original pieces of music in various styles. We'll explore how AI can compose melodies, harmonies, and even generate musical accompaniments.

- This technology holds immense potential for musicians, composers, and even the gaming industry.

Chapter 7: Generative AI for Drug Discovery and Material Science

Beyond creative endeavors, generative AI is making waves in scientific fields. Here, we'll explore how it's accelerating scientific breakthroughs.

- **7.1 Molecule Generation for Pharmaceuticals:**
  - Drug discovery is a time-consuming and expensive process. Generative AI can design new molecules with desired properties, potentially leading to faster development of life-saving drugs.

- We'll explore how models can virtually synthesize new molecules and predict their potential effectiveness against various diseases.

- **7.2 Material Design and Property Prediction**

  - Generative AI is transforming material science. We'll explore how models can design novel materials with specific properties, tailored for applications like solar panels or lightweight aircraft.

  - This technology can significantly accelerate material discovery and development, leading to advancements in various engineering fields.

Chapter 8: Generative AI for Other Applications

The potential applications of generative AI software are vast and ever-expanding. Here, we'll explore some additional areas where generative AI is making a significant impact.

- **8.1 Generative AI for Data Augmentation:**
    - Training machine learning models often requires vast amounts of data. Generative AI can be used to create synthetic data, effectively augmenting existing datasets.
    - This is particularly useful for applications where real-world data might be scarce or sensitive.

- **8.2 Generative AI for Natural Language Processing Tasks (Dialogue Systems, Machine Translation):**

  - Generative AI plays a crucial role in Natural Language Processing (NLP) tasks. We'll explore how models are used to develop chatbots that can hold more natural conversations and improve machine translation, enabling seamless communication across languages.

By exploring these diverse applications, you'll gain a deeper understanding of the transformative power of generative AI software and its potential

to revolutionize various aspects of our world.

I'd be glad to craft content in human form for the

remaining section:

Part 4: The Future of Generative AI

This section delves into the exciting yet thought-provoking future of generative AI. We'll explore the ethical considerations surrounding its development and delve into the cutting-edge advancements shaping the field.

Chapter 9: Ethical Considerations in Generative AI Development

- **9.1 Bias and Fairness in Generative Models:** Generative models, like any AI system, are susceptible to inheriting biases present in the data they're trained on. This section explores the potential for bias in generated content and how it can perpetuate social inequalities. We'll discuss strategies for mitigating bias in generative AI development, such as using diverse datasets and employing fairness metrics during training.

- **9.2 Mitigating the Risks of Generative AI:** The ability to create highly realistic content raises concerns about misuse. This section explores potential risks associated with generative AI, such as the creation of deepfakes for malicious purposes or the spread of misinformation. We'll discuss strategies for mitigating these risks, including developing

detection methods for deepfakes and

fostering responsible development practices.

Chapter 10: Future Trends and Advancements in Generative AI

The field of generative AI is constantly evolving. This section explores some of the exciting trends and advancements shaping the future of generative models.

- **10.1 Explainable and Controllable Generative Models:** One of the key challenges in generative AI is understanding how models arrive at their outputs. This section explores the development of explainable AI (XAI) techniques for generative models. With XAI, we can gain insights into the decision-making process of the model, fostering trust and enabling greater control over the generated content.

- **10.2 Generative AI for Real-world Applications:** The potential applications of generative AI are constantly expanding. This section explores some of the emerging and groundbreaking applications of generative AI in real-world scenarios. We might delve into areas like personalized education, where generative models can tailor learning experiences, or even scientific discovery, where AI can assist in tasks like protein

structure prediction.

By exploring these ethical considerations and

future trends, you'll gain a comprehensive

understanding of the evolving landscape of

generative AI and its potential impact on society.

www.ingramcontent.com/pod-product-compliance
Lightning Source LLC
LaVergne TN
LVHW051632050326
832903LV00033B/4715